Words Spoken Over You

From the Words of Jesus in Luke

Words Spoken Over You
From the Words of Jesus in Luke

Published by: **Incense Publishing, LLC**
PO Box 3001, Madison, MS 39110

This book is a book of prayers based on the words of Jesus in
the Holy Bible.

Incense Publishing books are available at special discounts
for bulk purchases. For more information, contact Incense
Publishing, LLC, Marketing Department, PO Box 3001,
Madison, MS 39110.

ISBN: 0988499428
ISBN-13: 9780988499423
ISBN: 9780988499423 (eBook)
Library of Congress Control Number: 2013940652
CreateSpace Independent Publishing Platform
North Charleston, South Carolina

FIRST EDITION

Words
Spoken
Over You

ROB LEWIS

Incense Publishing

Dedication

To my children, Anah, Tre, and Marie,
who are blessings from God to me and my wife, Linda.

Introduction

What if everyone in the world prayed for their children? And what if the very words of Jesus were turned into prayers for them and were spoken over them before God's throne?

Would the God of heaven and earth turn away and refuse to hear? Or would the very foundations of our world be shaken because God heard our pleas and answered them with great power and miracles?

The Bible is filled with examples of how the humble prayers of His servants parted waters, extinguished flames, released chains, devoured enemies, cured the sick, made people rise from the dead, and brought eternal salvation to the condemned.

There is no limit to what He can do for our children when we pray for them. He loves them more than we can ever know, and, for some reason, He has chosen to answer words spoken over them in prayer.

He will answer if we ask. So let us pray for them!

Introductory Prayer

Lord Jesus, as your words were the most complete anyone has ever spoken, make these prayers complete for my children.

Chapter 1

Luke 2:49 Young Jesus in His Father's House

Lord, may my children always be found in your temple, in your presence, in your counsel. As sons and daughters, may they long to be with you, their Father.

Luke 4:4, 4:8, 4:12 The Temptation of Jesus

- May the defense of scripture protect my children from temptation. Let it be in their hearts—strong, fortified, and effective in combat.
- May they not be drawn to the bread of this world or be deceived by eating it but live on every word that proceeds from your mouth.
- Prevent the potential idols of this world from robbing you of rightful position as their Lord. May they worship and serve you alone.
- May they not put you to the test.

Luke 4:18-19, 21, 23-27 Jesus Rejected in Nazareth

Pour your Spirit out on my children. Give them your words to preach the good news to the poor, to proclaim freedom to the prisoners, to recover sight to the blind, to release the oppressed, and to proclaim the year of the Lord's favor.

May they recognize your presence when scripture is fulfilled.

Chapter 2

Luke 4:35 Jesus Drives Out an Evil Spirit

Lord, destroy the works of the devil through the work you have given my children. And through them, may the power of your Holy Spirit muzzle unclean spirits and liberate people who are constantly irritated by them.

Luke 4:43 Jesus Sent to Preach to Many

Like you, Lord, may my children not live to themselves but bring the light of your Gospel to many.

Luke 5:4, 10 The Catching of Many Fish

Lord, you are the Master of the seas of men. Enter into each child's ship and by your instruction, power, and understanding of man, calm their fears and lead them to catch many sons and daughters for you in the days ahead.

Luke 5:13-14 Man with Leprosy

In a leprous world polluted with sin, may my children consider it worth falling before you each day in humble thankfulness of your pardoning mercy and renewing grace.

By your example, who entered into a world of sin and showed how low you would stoop to carry out the Father's will, may my children see no boundary, high or low, to engage your plan.

Jesus, our healing was your will. Now that we are healed, give my children a desire to bring your sacrifice into recognition, where you stand to receive glory, honor, and praise.

Chapter 3

Luke 5:20, 22-24 Jesus Heals a Paralytic

The forgiveness of sins is the most prized crown that you brought—the crown that makes men righteous. Continue to build in my children a growing desire to speak your truth in power.

Luke 5:27, 31-32 Calling of Levi

Use my children in calling the sick to repentance wherever they may be found.

Luke 5:34-39 Jesus Questioned about Fasting

Lord, challenge my children in the way you know they will best respond. You did not force your disciples to fast in their early walk, nor did you rebuke the sinners at their gathering when you called Levi. You knew what was right for the time and did not put new wine in old wineskins. Each of my children is in a special time in his or her walk with you. Give them the encouragement they need in your meeting with them today.

Luke 6:3-5, 8-10 Jesus, Lord of the Sabbath

Jesus, you came to fulfill the law and not to destroy it. Your acts of kindness extended to the Sabbath. Extend your kindness to my children. Bring to them sustenance and healing.

Chapter 4

Luke 6:20-26 Blessings and Woes

- Bless them when they are poor; may theirs be the kingdom of heaven.
- Bless them when they hunger; may they be satisfied.
- Bless them when they weep; may their tears turn to laughter.
- Bless them when they are hated by men, when they are excluded, insulted, and their name rejected as evil because of you. May they rejoice in that day, knowing their reward from you is great.

Let my children not trust in the riches of this world. Let them not pride themselves in them nor make them a sanctuary.

May their appetites, desires, and gratifications not be in empty worldly senses but instead be filled with you.

Luke 6:27-36 Love for Enemies

Father in heaven, provide to my children the ability to overcome their human nature and mimic your nature. Your ways are contrary to their natural thoughts and behavior. You love your enemies. You bless those who speak evil of you. Lord Jesus, you were not extreme in demanding your right when it was denied or rigorous in revenging a wrong when it was done to you. As the opportunities come to my children, give them the ability to continually repeat your nature: to repeat kindness and blessing, to bear no malice, to speak no ill, and to expect nothing in return.

Chapter 5

Luke 6:37-42 Judging Others

Lord, provide to my children a giving and forgiving spirit. Let them give and forgive generously in a measure equal to your measure to them.

Give them sight to see their own injustices and a willingness to correct them. Protect them from blindly leading others.

Jesus, you were never ambitious for the things of this world. You established this principle as Master. Help my children to never expect more from this world than you, their Master, did.

Let my children not be spies of the small faults of others but help them understand their own and be qualified to be of service to the souls of others.

Luke 6:43-45 A Tree and Its Fruit

The roots of human hearts are vicious, vile, and vulgar, Lord. But somehow, by your saving power in Christ, they sprout a branch from the Vine that bears beautiful, eternal fruit. May my children's hearts reveal them, Lord. May their hearts reveal the treasures within by word and deed.

Chapter 6

Luke 6:46-49 The Wise and Foolish Builders

Father of safety, men build their foundations on hopeless
ground. There the soil lacks any ability to hold against the
raging winds and tides. By hearing and putting Christ's words
into practice, grant to my children a spiritual house, able and
secure for the trials appointed to them as part of your earthly
work.

Luke 7:9 Faith of the Centurion

Faith of the Centurion is uncommon among those who are
your disciples. May my children's faith in the coming years
be transformed in such a way as to gain your notice because of
its uncommon heights so that whatever they ask for in your
name will be given to them. Yet, like the Centurion, may their
approach to you be in a humility that is equally uncommon.

Luke 7:13-14 Jesus Raises a Widow's Son

Lord Jesus, your words to the widow were simple and full of
compassion—*"Don't cry."* Her loss was great: an only son. Your
words to the dead man were simple, too—*"Young man, I say to
you, get up!"* Simplicity, compassion, and power accompany each
other in your order of things. May they accompany the ministry
you have given my children, too, and may many dead souls rise
to spiritual life.

Chapter 7

Luke 7:22-28 Jesus and John the Baptist

Everyone looking asks the question John did, *"Are you the Messiah, or should we look for another?"* Evidence of your Messiahship came from the blind receiving sight, the lame walking, those with leprosy being cured, the deaf hearing, the dead being raised, and the good news being preached to the poor. Validation to the world that you are the Lamb of God came from your resurrection. Lord, make my children faithful and effective messengers of this good news! Like John, make them a people of steadiness and unshaken constancy, not reeds swayed by the wind or indulgers of luxury. Let them strive to be one of whom you said, *"...among those born of woman there is no one greater than John."*

Luke 7:31-35 Jesus Compares the Generation

Father, help my children persuade those unconcerned about their everlasting peace and eternity of their souls to be serious about who you are. May they reach those who sit at the marketplace like children playing with worldly things, unable to see the gravity of the message they ignore and find unimportant. Help my children awaken them out of their security.

Chapter 8

Luke 7:40-50 Jesus Anointed by a Sinful Woman

Jesus, may my children be those who love much, who have a deep sorrow and humiliation for their sins but gladly seek the opportunity to confess them before you.

Luke 8:5-15 Parable of the Sower

Lord Jesus, your people are at great advantage to be instructed by you, for unto them the secrets of the kingdom have been given. May my children's thankfulness overflow from this privilege. Let them covet to earnestly know your true intent and the full extent of your Word. Let them be inquisitive and acquaint themselves with its mystery. May they be led into the light, and lead others into the light, by the Father of lights.

May my children be preparers of soil, sowers of seed, and a hindrance to the enemy who comes to steal. May they be to the careless hearer of the Gospel a sweeter song; to the one who heeds it only for the present, a repeating song; to the one who falls away during trials, a smiling song; and to the one entangled by the cares of this life, a freeing song.

Protect them from the love of ease and pleasure, from the lawful delights too much indulged in, and from the pollutions that hinder fruit from full ripening. Burn the sources of practiced dangers, drive away competing perils, and cut off their diseased limbs that threaten a healthy tree.

Chapter 9

Luke 8:16-18 A Lamp on a Stand

Father, give my children passion of you and for you. In turn, may they be people whose light shines its full length and spectrum, so where they have, more will be given and not taken from them.

Luke 8:19-21 Jesus's Mother and Brothers

By preferring you to their nearest relation, allow my children to be your nearest and dearest.

Luke 8:22, 25 Jesus Calms the Storm

Jesus, as you lead my children to the other side of the lake, let their faith not fail in the storms. Let fear, pain, and apparent death not expose a lacking of their faith, but may they uncover the abundance of it.

Luke 8:30, 39 Healing of Demon-Possessed Man

Father, those who are led by Satan are furiously deposed. They are many and bind many with the cords of fear and hate. As instruments of your power and love, speak to Satan's government through my children and powerfully command the freeing of captured souls.

To those who are rescued, may my children participate in making them standing monuments in their communities and publishers of what great good you have done.

Chapter 10

Luke 8:45-46, 48, 50 A Sick Woman and a Dead Girl

Lord Jesus, it was not to your complaint that power sprang
from you to a desperate woman of faith but to your delight.
May my children be communicators of the news that you are an
overflowing fountain that can never be drained. Help them to
practice her bold and daring faith.

Amazing Lord, it was not in your mind to call a mortician for
the little girl but to call her soul to return and her body back to
life. May my children extend their hands and reach many souls
out of death and into life.

Luke 9:3-5 Jesus Sends Out the Twelve

Lord, you have sent my children to do good to both soul
and body. Let them claim your authority with amazing and
convincing proof that you are the Messiah.

Luke 9:13-14 Jesus Feeds the Five Thousand

As you were generous with what little you had (five loaves and
two fish), help my children to be generous with what they have.
May it multiply and feed the physical and spiritual necessities
of many.

Chapter 11

Luke 9:18, 20, 22-27 Peter's Confession of Christ

Jesus, there is great confusion in the world about who you are. Make my children voices that carry a message of clarity as to your true identity.

As for the crosses that are laid before them, help my children take them up in duty, having a contempt of the world and preference for salvation.

When the day comes for profit and loss to be balanced, may they be found faithful in that duty and ready to receive the crown of life.

Luke 9:35 Transfiguration

Father, you chose Jesus and set him at the center of the new covenant. Let my children's perceptions always be centered around what you have chosen.

Luke 9:41, 44 Healing of a Boy with an Evil Spirit

Lord, set a tireless compassionate state upon my children that resembles yours. Help them not be defective in relieving those afflicted with Satan's mischief.

Father of perfect will, after all the miracles your Son had performed and after all the interest of others he had served, it did not prevent him from dying in disgrace. Just as Jesus confronted the difficult reality of your will and laid down the temporal for the eternal, may my children copy this obedience to your perfect plan for them.

Chapter 12

Luke 9:48, 50 Who Will Be the Greatest

Children are precious to you, Lord. Help my children to welcome all your little ones.

May it be their ambition to be the least and servants to all here on earth.

Luke 9:58-62 The Cost of Following Jesus

Lord Jesus, build in my children a holy contempt of the world and an attraction to the poverty you lived.

Because service to the Gospel is urgent, let them not defer in following you, even for seemingly reasonable excuses.

Luke 10:2-24 Jesus Sends Out the Seventy-Two

The harvest fields are plentiful, Lord. You have sent my children to be ploughers of those fields. By the power of your Holy Spirit, give to them the message that saves souls day by day.

May your peace go with them and rest upon those who welcome them.

Give them power to overcome all the power of the enemy and yet let them not rejoice that spirits are subject to them but rather that their names are written in heaven.

Grant a holy thankfulness and a joyful heart to well up within them, that though they were found to be in such lowly estate you revealed the hidden things to them. May they be awakened by the great advantage of living in the New Testament light.

Chapter 13

Luke 10:26, 28, 30-37 Parable of the Good Samaritan

Father, help my children to consider you above all they consider. Let their love for you be complete within their beings, in their hearts, souls, strength, and in their minds.

Let not human corruption convince them to exclude people as their neighbors. Give them a compassion for the needy with action—a compassion that submits its energy to others without judgment on their deserving merit.

Luke 10:41-42 At the Home of Martha and Mary

Jesus, help my children not to be encumbered with the distractions of worldliness when something more commendable to your kingdom is present.

Luke 11:2-11 Jesus Teaches the Disciples to Pray

Lord Jesus, grant to my children a will to be imitators and emulators of your zeal for prayer. Teach them the meaning of prayer; excite and quicken their souls to it; direct them in what to pray for; provide them grace that they may acceptably serve you in the duty of prayer; give them mouths of wisdom, that they may use the proper words before your throne.

Help them to ascribe honor to your name; to await in great expectation your kingdom to come; to depend on your daily portion of bread; to plead your forgiveness of their sins and the ability to forgive others; to lean on you to protect them from the charming temptations laid before them.

Let them not be faint in praying but continually asking, fervently seeking, and strenuously knocking because all these things please you.

Chapter 14

Luke 11:17-28 Jesus and Beelzebub

Lord, with my children as instruments of your power, disarm Satan with your Word and break the power of sin and corruption in unbelieving hearts. Let those whom you have converted understand by whom they were freed and be taken into your service.

Make my children hearers and doers of your Word. May they be lights of understanding to others that your blessing covers those who both hear and obey.

Luke 11:29-32 Sign of Jonah

Lord Jesus, the greatest and most convincing sign that you are the savior of the world is your resurrection. As your disciples, may my children be bearers of this sign to the ends of the earth.

Luke 11:33-36 Lamp of the Body

Father, you have provided an abundance of light in the world. Your Word is plentiful in print, speech, and deed, yet the eyes of people see it not. Help my children to be effective at bringing perception and clarity to those who have eyes and do not see.

Chapter 15

Luke 11:39-52 Six Woes

Jesus, give my children confidence to call out absurdity in religion, where the practices of man take precedence over a true devotion to you.

- Help them not to be neglectors of justice and love.
- Protect them from pride, vanity, and the wanted affections of men.
- Clean from them the sins of hypocrisies and superficial appearances.
- Guide them away from teaching burdensome law and ignoring mercy.
- May all that they are and all that they teach resemble those whom you sent to bring your Word and not those who murdered them.
- Help them to use the key of knowledge of the Gospel given them to open up and spread it to many.

Luke 12:2-12 Warnings and Encouragements

Lord, your great caution was against hypocrisy in leaders. Give to my children a healthy understanding and fear of you such that it makes them Christ-like and avoid being Pharisee-like.

If you have their hairs numbered then so are their tears, their days in pain, their hours in sorrow, and their drops of blood shed for your sake. Help them to understand your encouraging love.

All of mankind will be owned or disowned on whether they have owned or disowned you. May my children lead others to confidence in owning you.

Father, you sufficiently furnish the trials we face with your Holy Spirit. Through Him, provide what my children need on that day. Though they may suffer, may the cause of Christ not suffer. Give them the words and actions of a faithful testimony and a strong confession.

Chapter 16

Luke 12:14-21 Parable of the Rich Fool

Jesus, you knew the things of this world would not satisfy the soul. The temporal things made of physical matter stand deficient in meeting the needs of an eternal spiritual soul meant for your kingdom. Protect my children from finding worth in such inferior substances.

Help them not to want or store up what you did not want or store up. May there never be found in them a condition of hoarding.

Luke 12:22-34 Do Not Worry

Father, you provide for the lilies nutrients in the dirt and a tiny root to absorb them, yet all the world's riches do not exceed their astounding beauty and captivating colors. Give my children the faith of these little fading and perishable creations who neither toil or spin over their provisions. May their thoughts and minds be spent on the cares of your heavenly kingdom and work.

Let them sell what possessions they see as superfluous or a hindrance to your service and give them to the poor, desiring you as their treasure and exceeding reward.

Chapter 17

Luke 12:35-48 Watchfulness

Jesus, the time of your coming is uncertain. May my children be found as expectant and waiting servants in a posture ready to be received by you. Help them to be witnesses to the unfaithful of the dreadful reckoning that awaits them.

Luke 12:49-53 Not Peace but Division

Lord, you made it clear the Gospel would not meet with universal welcome but with division—divisions that reach continents, countries, states, counties, cities, and even families. Let my children not be promisers of peace on earth but people who prepare the sheep to be sent forth among wolves.

Luke 12:54-59 Interpreting the Times

Jesus, the ruin of men when you walked the earth was that they did not recognize that their long-awaited Messiah was speaking to them. Help my children to be wise in discerning the times.

The world has but a brief time in which to respond to you, Lord. May my children be those who help people contend with you before it is too late and the law condemns them.

Chapter 18

Luke 13:2-9 Repent or Perish

There will be a remarkable resemblance of the fate of those who did not repent and perished thousands of years ago and those who do not repent today and perish. May my children repeat the loud calls of repentance to this unbelieving generation.

Lord Jesus, as you intercede for the barren fig trees of the world and patiently wait for leaves to produce blossoms and blossoms to produce fruit, make my children effective intercessors like you: people who are devoted to seeking and pleading mercy for others and ready to fertilize and care for their roots.

Luke 13:12-13, 5-16 Crippled Woman Healed on the Sabbath

Jesus, as you were here to attend to the best interest of the souls of men, you attended well to their bodies too. Grant to my children many opportunities to care for the needs of people inflicted with infirmities of soul and body. Allow them freedom from criticism for doing these merciful acts.

Chapter 19

Luke 13:18-20 Parable of the Mustard Seed and Yeast

Father, make my children effective planters of your seeds. You made these seeds small and easily transportable. Help my children to carry many with them along life's journey and be generous in their plantings.

Lord, yeast is microscopic, is carried by the air, and needs little water and nutrients to grow. As the yeast of the Gospel proceeds from my children's hands in silence, may it infiltrate the world without force or violence yet subdue and vanquish the armies of Satan.

Luke 13:24-30 The Narrow Door

Father of salvation, allow my children to be those who help people awaken out of a lazy seeking of their eternal destiny and make every effort to enter through the narrow door. Give them the ability to quicken hearts, strengthen convictions, and guide others to think of the distinguishing day that is coming.

Luke 13:32-35 Jesus's Sorrow for Jerusalem

Lord, make my children persuaders of the unwilling, those who guide them as chicks under your willing and caring wings.

Chapter 20

Luke 14:3-4 Jesus at a Pharisee's House

Jesus, help my children not be afraid of those who would cast stones at them for doing good. Yet let them do their good in the least offensive way.

Make them people who are content with the lowly seats of the humble.

Let their motive of social hospitality be one that does not seek a return.

Luke 14:6-24 Parable of the Great Banquet

Father, your banquet is ready, and your house is open. Let my children be tireless distributors of your invitations. Let them carry with them a convincing message that the season of grace is at hand and that its value far surpasses any worldly possession.

Luke 14:26-35 Cost of Being a Disciple

Though my children may never be crucified, may they bear their crosses as if they always expect to.

Continually reassure my children that the cost of discipleship is worth far more than what they might lose: their reputations, relationships, estates, liberties, and lives.

Lord, you have made salt one of the most important minerals in preserving and sustaining life. Above all its characteristics, it is useful and makes other things useful. Help my children to make themselves useful minerals, preserving and sustaining others through the life you give them.

Chapter 21

Luke 15:4-7 Parable of the Lost Sheep

Lost sheep are frightened and exposed, Lord. Though they may have departed away from you on their own, they are very precious to you. Make my children searchers and rescuers of your lost sheep.

Luke 15:8-10 Parable of the Lost Coin

As you expended great energy searching for lost souls, may my children find it worth their energy to search for them too.

Luke 15:11-32 Parable of the Lost Son

Father, when you welcome home great sinners, may my children be servants who find the occasion one of rejoicing.

Luke 16:1-15 Parable of the Shrewd Manager

Father, give my children wisdom to be diligent, industrious, and honest with what you have given them. Help them to employ their riches here on earth with an eye to the eternal.

Chapter 22

Luke 16:16-18 Further Teaching

Lord, you have opened the New Covenant to great throngs of
people without limitation, yet the Law remains steady. Grant to
my children a holy understanding of both in light of the Gospel
of grace.

What men permitted in the Law by corrupt appetites and
carnal passions, the Gospel no longer allows. Give my children
wisdom in scoping out these practices and bringing them to
light.

Luke 16:19-31 The Rich Man and Lazarus

Lord, those who are fast asleep in sin and without Christ are
not easily awakened. Life's pleasures anesthetize them further
and further into dreamy states, making them unable to see
the pending danger of their eternal reality. Give my children a
special gift in bringing those asleep to consciousness.

Chapter 23

Luke 17:1-10 Sin, Faith, and Duty

Father, let my children's fingerprints not be found in the cause of others' sins. May they be diligent, watchful, and take great caution in preventing offenses, especially to your little ones.

Subside their passions and prevent their spirits from being provoked in anger at others who sin against them. Let them not speak at all, or at least not ill-advised, during such collisions that give them injury. And though the wounds may be many and travel deep in their flesh, may their spirit of forgiveness be such a healing balm that forgiveness comes quick, often, and remains permanent.

If it is fit to be done for your glory and for the confirmation of the Gospel truth, let my children have the faith of whatever small seed is necessary to uproot any tree and throw it into the sea.

Help my children to fill up their time with the duty of your work that is appointed to them so that the end of one task becomes the beginning of another. Let them look to you in humility and find comfort in the yokes they bear for the cause of Christ.

Chapter 24

Luke 17:14, 17-19 Ten Healed of Leprosy

Jesus, help my children to call out to you for the curing of their infirmities, to yield to your ways and methods of healing, and to be rich in publicly giving you thanks and glory after being made whole.

Luke 17:20-37 The Coming of the Kingdom of God

Lord, the current manifestation of your kingdom resides within people's repentant hearts. It is here, now, among us for a short time. Give my children an open door for the Gospel of repentance to be preached.

When your kingdom does come to earth in physical form and you are revealed in power, it will be a sudden, unexpected, and frightening event for many. Guide my children to be faithful sons and daughters of Noah and Lot by preparing their Christian family for that day and warning unbelievers of what is certain to come.

Luke 18:1-8 Parable of the Persistent Widow

Father, help my children to be persistent in prayer and confident in your justice, always communicating with you in a constant stream of thought and word.

Chapter 25

Luke 18:9-14 Parable of the Pharisee and the Tax Collector

Lord, let them not be exalters of themselves before you in prayer. May their presence and speech be of humility.

Luke 18:15-17 The Little Children and Jesus

Jesus, none are too young to be brought to you. Make my children encouragers of parents in bringing their children to you.

Luke 18:18-30 Parable of the Rich Ruler

Lord, men think themselves innocent. They know no more evil of themselves than the Pharisees or the rich ruler. Protect my children from acquainting themselves closely with this thinking.

Riches can be a spiritual hindrance. Help my children to possess a spiritual mind, one that sees no loss in what they have left or laid out in this world.

Luke 18:31-34 Jesus Predicts Their Death

Jesus, unlike the rich ruler, you gave everything. And because of your prior knowledge of suffering, you carried with you the constant torment of its pain before its happening to satisfy the justice of our sin. Help my children to see the contrast in your willingness and mimic it.

Chapter 26

Luke 18:41-43 Blind Beggar Receives Sight

Lord, as the blind man made use of better eyes to understand it was Jesus of Nazareth passing by, help my children to inquire of others with their weaker functions.

Let them take note and copy the beggar's faith and fervency in you, an able and merciful King.

Luke 19:5-6,9-10 Zacchaeus the Tax Collector

Lord, you have a remnant among all sorts—even sinners like Zacchaeus. Help my children to open the kingdom to everyone, as you did. Let them not take offense of those you select.

Grant them a curiosity of you that sincerely desires your company, such that they climb trees like children to catch a glimpse of you.

As you invited yourself to Zacchaeus's house, give my children the boldness to invite you into people's hearts.

Like Zacchaeus, help my children to evidence the sincerity of their faith and repentance through good deeds.

Luke 19:12-27 Parable of the Ten Minas

Father, grant my children an urgency in utilizing the gifts provided to them to conduct their business. Let them expect power from your expected service and help them to produce great gain from it. May they be diligent in giving you the glory.

Protect them from protecting their stock. Help them rather to risk some pain, some expense, and some hazard for the gain of the kingdom.

Chapter 27

Luke 19:30-31, 40, 42-44 The Triumphal Entry

Like the owners of the colt, when there is occasion for your service, grant my children an open hand to all their possessions.

Let my children be the rocks that cry out in praise of you if the world halts.

Jesus, your visitation has occurred, and unlike the temporal fall of Jerusalem, which perished less than forty years after that day, an eternal fall is soon to occur. Help my children to bring multitudes into the vineyard at this eleventh hour.

Luke 19:46 Jesus at the Temple

Jesus, you had great zeal for your temple. It was a house of prayer, set apart for communion with God. May my children have like zeal for their temples (bodies).

Luke 20:3, 8 Jesus's Authority Questioned

Lord, let it not be a strange thing to my children that their spreading of the Gospel is disputed, knowing Satan will go to great lengths to extinguish his greatest threat.

Give them great power to preach and teach with authority, and let none honestly deny by whose authority they do these things.

Luke 20:9-16, 17-18 Parable of the Tenants

Father, help my children to take great care in being tenants of your vineyard. Let them someday be able to present great fruits from it.

The Stone the builders rejected was their Savior. You are rejected in this generation, too, Lord, but though the hearts of men are fully set to do evil, let my children be convincing messengers of the sin men are about to commit in denying you—and of its consequences.

Chapter 28

Luke 20:24-25 Paying Taxes to Caesar

Jesus, provide heavenly evasion for my children when enemies try to entrap them in a snare.

In civil matters, let my children submit themselves to civil powers, but in sacred matters may you, and you alone, be King.

Luke 20:34-38 Resurrection and Marriage

Lord, men load your truth with difficulties. They subvert it and weaken it to their satisfaction. Help my children to unwind these false beliefs and straighten them to understanding.

As you did, Lord, let them effectively teach the differences between the visible world and the invisible one.

Luke 20:41-47 Whose Son Is the Christ?

Jesus, you are the root and offspring of David. By your human nature, you were his offspring, a lineage of his family tree. By divine nature, you were his root, the very creator of his being. Let there be no contradiction in my children's perceptions of your nature, as there was none in yours.

Father, protect my children from using their religion as a cloak and cover for sins.

Luke 21:3-4 Widow's Offering

Lord, you have your eye on what my children contribute out of their earnings. Let them be found as the widow who gave the most famous offering the world has ever known. May their examples, like hers, promote many to give in the same way.

Chapter 29

Luke 21:6, 8-36 Signs of the End of the Age

Lord, help my children to create such communion with you in whatever place they attend where your Word is preached that people speak not of the place itself. Let them find their mouths speaking of your presence, the ordinances administered in it, and the intimacy the people share with each other and with you.

Make my children spotters of false prophets and prophecies and protectors of your flock from them.

Father, the day may come for my children to suffer for their faith, when the men of this age lay hands on them, beat them, and deliver them to the courts and prisons, when they are brought before kings and governors on account of your name. On that day, if it comes, let them not worry about themselves or what they should say. Though pain comes sharply, let their words bloom ever brighter by the direction of your Spirit.

During such times as the end of the age, men's hearts will fail them, Lord. Help my children's not to.

I pray that they may escape all that is about to happen and that they may be able to stand before you.

Chapter 30

Luke 22:8-28 The Last Supper

In preparation for the Passover, you sent Peter and John to find the house by different means. Instead of "Go to such and such a house" or "Go to such and such a street," you said, *"As you enter the city a man carrying a jar of water will meet you."* Let my children not be in the habit of questioning what may seem like "strange" instructions, but let their habit be obeying them.

Jesus, you so eagerly desired to eat the Passover meal with your disciples, though it was a prologue before you suffered. Your desire to do the will of the Father is without condition; whether suffering or joy should come, you eagerly desire it. Give to my children this extinct and forgotten type of desire.

As they remember you in times of the Lord's Supper, may their thoughts and prayers be acceptable in your sight.

Lord, grave betrayals still occur on this cursed land we walk. May my children's attitudes toward their betrayers be of sorrow from what they have done to themselves and to you rather than anger of what was done to them.

Protect them from the contests of earthly dignity and dominion, from positioning themselves to the left or right of you in your kingdom. Let them leave external pomp and power to the sons of this world and concentrate on being sons and daughters of God.

Lord Jesus, before and during times of Satan's sifting, pray to the Father for my children. Pray that their faith may not fail and that, after their time of testing is complete, they may use its lessons to strengthen their brothers and sisters.

Chapter 31

Luke 22:39-6 Jesus Prays on the Mount of Olives

Father, may my children not fall into temptation during their gravest moments or their most exalted ones. Help them to recognize when these times are upon them and be more diligent in their protections.

Luke 22:48, 51-53 Jesus Arrested

When the mobs were upon you, Lord Jesus, you did not cower or shrink, nor did you allow violence against your captors. Give my children such an attitude toward the Father's will as yours, that all their thoughts and senses conform to it.

Luke 22:67-70 Jesus before the Chief Priests and Teachers of the Law

From your own lips you condemned yourself when asked if you were the Son of God. Your answer was, *"You are right in saying that I am."* Give my children such confidence and conviction in who you are that they would rather send themselves to a cross than deny it.

Luke 23:3 Jesus before Pilate

When asked if you were the King of the Jews, your answer was, *"Yes, it is as you say."* Jesus, you are King of kings and Lord of lords. As subjects in your kingdom, give my children authority to carry out your bidding.

Chapter 32

Luke 23:9 Jesus before Herod

Jesus, you gave no answer to Herod's many questions. Let my children know when to be silent.

Luke 23:28-31, 34, 43 The Crucifixion

Lord, you had an eye on the coming destruction of Jerusalem and the miseries that would soon come to her. Help my children to warn the daughters of this age of the coming destruction.

Jesus, you made intersession for your transgressors in your darkest hour. Help my children to have such affection for sinners that your image shines bright through their beings, and they share in this unnatural mystery of forgiveness.

Lord, the two thieves crucified with you reveal your timeless mercy even in a time of great agony. You did not speak ill of the one who railed at you, nor did you deny grace to the one who sought you. Let my children's mercy stretch beyond this known world and deep into eternity.

Chapter 33

Luke 23:46 Jesus's Death

Father, someday there may be a separation of body and spirit for my children (if your second coming does not occur first). On that day, receive their spirits into your presence and into your glory.

Luke 24:17, 19, 25–26 Road to Emmaus

Lord, there are many more prophecies yet to be fulfilled in scripture. Instruct my children in them and give them a quickness to believe them as they are fulfilled.

Luke 24:36–39, 41, 44 Jesus Appears to the Disciples

Jesus, may your peace be with my children.

Let not their hearts be troubled within them nor doubts rise in their minds.

What has been written in the Law of Moses, the Prophets, and the Psalms has come to pass: that the Christ would suffer and be raised on the third day, and repentance and forgiveness of sins would be preached in His name to all nations, beginning in Jerusalem. By the power of your Spirit, make my children such a witness to your truth that great multitudes are brought from darkness and into the light.

Acknowledgments

No words can express my gratitude and thankfulness to the Lord for Matthew Henry, a man who sat at a little wooden desk in the early 1700s and wrote his celebrated commentary, *An Exposition of the Old and New Testament*. Due to his faithfulness hundreds of years ago, much help was derived from his commentary in the writing of these prayers.

Also by Rob Lewis

To Carry the Cross — Co-Authored with

Rick Williams

www.ingramcontent.com/pod-product-compliance
Lightning Source LLC
Chambersburg PA
CBHW020516030426
42337CB00011B/412